DATE DUE			
SE 23 '91			
JE 21 '95			
JY 26 '95			
JY 13 '96			
JY 31 '96			

Jet Watercraft

John Martin

Capstone Press

MINNEAPOLIS

Capstone Press • 2440 Fernbrook Lane • Minneapolis, MN 55447

Editorial Director   John Coughlan
Managing Editor   John Martin
Copy Editor   Theresa Early
Editorial Assistant   Michelle Wood

Library of Congress Cataloging-in-Publication Data

Martin, John, 1968-
  Jet watercraft / John Martin.
     p. cm.-- (Cruisin')
  Includes bibliographical references and index.
  ISBN 1-56065-201-2 (lib. bdg.)
  1. Jet boats--Juvenile literature. [1. Jet boats.]   I. Title.
II. Series.
VM348.5.M37 1994
623.8'231--dc20   93-45538
                                                CIP
                                                 AC
ISBN: 1-56065-201-2

99 98 97 96 95 94   8 7 6 5 4 3 2 1

Table of Contents

Riding a jet watercraft really lets you experience the sensation of speed.

Chapter 1

Ready, Set, Go!

Sit back and picture yourself skimming across the water at high speed.

Wind rushes past you. The sound of a roaring motor fills your ears. You can feel the bounce of the craft on the rough water.

If you have ever been in a speedboat you know how fast and exciting it can be. Even speeds we think are slow on land somehow seem much faster on water.

Speedboats are fun. But a better way to feel the excitement of water sports is to put yourself behind the handlebars of a jet watercraft.

The smile on this pilot's face shows just how fun operating a jet watercraft can be.

Now imagine yourself racing through the waves at speeds up to 60 miles (96.5 kilometers) per hour. Wind-driven spray beats against your face and body.

You steer your craft into razor-sharp turns and over tall waves. You feel the speed, the ease of movement, and the excitement that only a jet watercraft can give you.

Jet watercraft can make razor-sharp turns at speed.

A skilled pilot performs an impressive stunt on a stand-up jet watercraft.

Chapter 2

About Jet Watercraft

The Japanese company Kawasaki introduced the Jet Ski in the early 1970s. Since then, the sport of jet watercrafting has grown by leaps and bounds. Almost a dozen companies now make jet watercraft in many shapes and sizes. More than 40 different models are now available.

The original jet watercraft was designed to be driven by a standing pilot. It had no seat. The pilot stood behind a movable handlebar and leaned into the turns, much like a waterskier does.

Stand-up models are still popular, but the latest jet watercraft have seats. They are

A stand-up model (above) is meant to be operated by a single, standing pilot. A sit-down model (pictured below) is operated by a seated pilot and has room for more than one rider.

designed to be piloted sitting down. And while
the first jet watercraft could hold only one
rider, today's models are for one, two, or even
three riders.

Whatever their style, all jet watercraft have
one thing in common. On the water they offer
fast-paced, wet-and-wild fun.

What Is a Jet Watercraft?

The U.S. Coast Guard puts jet watercraft
into a group called "Class A inboard boats."
Jet watercraft, however, are very different from
most inboard boats.

Jet watercraft are much smaller. Stand-up
models measure about 85 inches (216
centimeters) long or less and are about 28 inches
(71 centimeters) wide.

Sit-down models are bigger. A typical sit-
down jet watercraft is about 110 inches (279
centimeters) long and 38 inches (97 centimeters)
wide.

You can not get *inside* a jet watercraft.
Instead, the pilot sits, kneels, or stands on a

platform. The watercraft has no sides to hold the pilot in.

This lets the pilots lean hard into the turns. Sometimes pilots lean so hard that their bodies touch the water.

Jet Power

Another special feature of jet watercraft is the internal propeller, or **impeller**. An area beneath the engine, the **intake**, pushes water

A pilot leans hard into a turn.

Sometimes pilots lean so hard that their bodies touch the water.

toward the impeller. The impeller draws water in and forces it out the back of the craft. This **jet propulsion** makes the craft move forward.

Because the propeller is enclosed, the pilot does not have to worry about sharp spinning blades when he or she climbs aboard or takes a spill.

Jet-Power Steering

Most boats use **rudders** to steer, but jet watercraft use a jet-propelled stream of water.

Directly behind the impeller is the **steering nozzle**. It is connected to the handlebars by a metal bar. The steering nozzle uses the rush of water to steer the craft.

Remember this when coming in to shore. Once you turn off the power, you no longer can steer the watercraft.

The Hull

The main body of a boat is called the **hull.** The jet watercraft hull is made of fiberglass. It is covered with a tough epoxy gel-coat, a hard coating that protects the hull from dents and scratches. The gel-coat gives the jet watercraft its bright shine.

The hull lets the craft float. It is in constant contact with the water. Most hulls have tracks on them, raised parallel ridges running the length of the hull. These make the craft more stable.

Ridges on the hulls of jet watercraft keep them stable during high-speed turns.

A Place for the Pilot

A jet watercraft has either a seat or a **footpad** for the pilot. Seats on jet watercraft can be narrow, like motorcycle seats, or wide, like snowmobile seats.

Jet watercraft seats are made of vinyl. They are filled with synthetic foam that does not rot when it gets wet. The seats help take the jolt out of rough water and waves.

The footpad is on the area of the hull where the pilot stands. It is covered with foam rubber to absorb shock from rough water. It also provides secure footing for the standing pilot.

Handlebars

All jet watercraft have handlebars. There are two types of handlebars—stationary and movable.

Stationary handlebars are set in place. They can be used in one position only. You can turn them to the left and right, like the handlebars on a bicycle, but you cannot raise or lower them. Most sit-down jet watercraft have this type of steering.

Sit-down jet watercraft have seats and stationary handlebars.

You can turn stationary handlebars to the left and right, but you cannot raise or lower them.

Most stand-up models of jet watercraft have movable handlebars. Pilots of this type of craft start in a kneeling position and then stand up. They need movable handlebars that can be used in both positions.

The Hood

The fiberglass shell that covers the engine is called the **hood**. The hood protects the engine from moisture. It also drowns out some of the motor's noise. Mechanics take the hood off when they need to work on the engine.

Safety equipment, such as a life vest, gloves, goggles and helmet, is needed when executing advanced tricks on jet watercraft.

Chapter 3

Getting Equipped

Like most fast sports, riding a jet watercraft is somewhat risky. To cut the chance of injury, good-quality gear is a must. Expert pilots do not ride without safety gear, and neither should you.

The Life Vest

The most important piece of equipment is the life vest or **PFD (personal flotation device)**.

A good PFD should do three things: keep you afloat if you fall into the water, cushion your fall, and keep you warm.

Piloting a jet watercraft is tiring. Treading water after a fall tires you even faster. A good

Safety equipment does not take away from the fun a jet watercraft can offer.

vest keeps you afloat and helps you to save your energy. If you become unconscious or seriously injured, the vest keeps your head above water.

In a hard fall, a good vest protects you from the water's impact. Some **wipeouts** are so serious they can cause you to lose your breath. A PFD can protect you from this. It can also save you from bumps, lumps, bruises, and scrapes.

PFDs protect you from **hypothermia**. Hypothermia occurs when your body temperature becomes dangerously lower than normal.

A good vest puts foam rubber between you and the water. The foam insulates your body and helps keep your body at its normal temperature. In very cold water, it's a good idea for a pilot to wear either a **wetsuit** or a **drysuit** to insulate his or her entire body.

Gloves

Wear gloves to protect your hands from soreness and blisters. Jet watercraft shops sell gloves specially designed for the sport, but waterski gloves work well, too.

Goggles and Sunglasses

It can be hard to keep your vision clear in all the water and wind a watercraft stirs up. To help you see, you should strap on a pair of goggles or wear sunglasses. If you decide to wear sunglasses, be sure to use a "leash" so you do not lose them if you fall.

Helmets

More and more smart pilots are wearing helmets. Although helmets are required only of people who race jet watercraft, it is good for all riders to wear helmets. You'll be glad you did if you ever take a serious fall or crash into another craft.

You should take it easy when first learning to ride a jet watercraft.

Chapter 4

Learning to Ride

Learning to ride a jet watercraft is like learning to ride a bike. It takes a little time to learn to balance, but after that it's easy.

Getting Aboard

Sit-down jet watercraft are generally wider and more stable than stand-up models. Getting aboard them is easy. Simply walk the craft out into waist-deep water. Climb onto the craft from the back and then onto the seat. Be careful not to rock the craft too much.

Starting out on a stand-up model is a bit more tricky because it requires better balance.

One false move and you could be thrown into the handlebars. Ouch!

To board a stand-up jet watercraft, place one knee on the end of the footpad. Grab the handlebars and face forward. Let your other knee drag in the water. This helps you balance until you get going.

Most jet watercraft have a plastic tether cord that shuts down the engine when the cord is pulled out. If the pilot falls off the watercraft he can pull the cord and prevent a "runaway."

Look for the coiled cord just under the handlebars, and clip it securely to your life vest.

Start Your Engine

The pilot starts the motor by pulling out the choke lever and pressing the start button. Choking the engine gives it more gas. Push the choke in after the engine runs for a while.

Like snowmobiles, jet watercraft have a thumb throttle that sticks out from the handlebar on the right. The thumb throttle controls the amount of fuel that goes to the engine.

The harder you press the thumb throttle, the faster you will go. But wait until you feel comfortable on a jet watercraft before pushing the throttle too hard.

And You're Off!

When you first start a jet watercraft, the engine is **idling**. This means that the engine is running but the watercraft is not moving. To go forward, squeeze the throttle slowly. But before you do, check your path to make sure it's clear.

Now push the throttle harder so that you can **plane**. Planing describes the craft going so fast that it is mostly out of the water. A planing jet watercraft can travel at speeds up to 60 miles (96.5 kilometers) per hour.

Since sit-down watercraft are more stable and easier to ride than stand-up models, you might be tempted to go fast immediately. Be careful.

During your first ride on a stand-up model, stay in the kneeling position to get a feel for the ride.

When you think you are ready, you can learn to stand. Stay on one knee. Pull your strongest leg forward. Plant that foot toward the front of the pad. Then use this leg to pull your entire body into a standing position.

To maintain proper balance, place your feet shoulder-width apart. If you lose your balance—and you probably will—just "bail out" into the water.

Turning

One of the things that makes jet watercraft piloting so much fun is turning. You can make your turns razor-sharp. Be careful, though, because you can be thrown from your craft while making a turn.

Lean in the direction you are turning. This is especially important on stand-up jet watercraft.

With a little practice you will be on your feet in no time.

Stopping

Jet watercraft do not have brakes. To stop, you release the throttle. The craft will sink into the water. The more the craft sinks, the more the craft's hull will **drag** in the water.

Drag simply and effectively slows the watercraft, and it quickly comes to a stop.

An expert rider loses his footing during a freestyle competition.

Chapter 5

Jet Watercraft Competitions

When you become a skilled pilot you might consider competing on your jet watercraft. The three major types of jet watercraft competitions are **slalom racing**, **closed-course racing**, and **freestyle competition**.

Slalom Racing

In slalom racing, each racer speeds through a course of 10 **buoys**. The racer who finishes the course in the shortest time wins. To keep

up his or her speed, a racer leans hard into the turns around the buoys. Racers lean way out over the water.

Closed-Course Racing

In closed-course competitions, several pilots race around buoys at the same time. The first to reach the finish line is the winner.

Freestyle competition allows riders to be creative and try new things.

Closed-course racing is more like combat than a race. Racers cut each other off and sometimes even collide. Because of this, closed-course racers always wear helmets and full protective gear.

Freestyle Competition

Freestyle pilots perform unusual and difficult tricks. Pilots are judged on the originality and difficulty of their tricks and how well they execute the tricks.

Freestyle pilots perform such tricks as the **submarine**, in which pilots make their watercraft dive nose first into the water. In the trick known as the **barefoot**, pilots hang their entire bodies away from the craft and ride over the water's surface with only their feet skimming the water.

Chapter 6
Playing It Safe

In recent years many people have spoken out against jet watercraft. Riders have too often bothered other boaters, made too much noise, and even injured swimmers.

For safety and courtesy, you should follow these simple rules:

1. Never ride so far from shore that you can't swim back.

2. Do not pilot through public swimming areas.

3. Watch out for floating objects that might be dangerous.

4. Be familiar with basic boating rules. Know the meaning of the different buoys, flags, and markers.

5. Never make noise that will disturb people on shore.

6. Always keep a safe distance between you and other craft.

Glossary

barefoot–a sharp move in which the pilot's feet skim out over the water

buoy–a floating object used to mark a channel or hazard

closed-course racing–racing on a marked course

drag–the force of water that slows a boat to a stop when the engine is off

drysuit–a close-fitting, waterproof suit worn by swimmers and divers in very cold water

footpad–a padded area on a stand-up jet watercraft where the pilot stands

freestyle competition–a contest of gymnastic moves and showy piloting

hull–the rigid outer covering of the jet watercraft

hypothermia–having a body temperature less than normal

idling–running, as an engine does, without using any of the energy for work

impeller–a set of blades that spin and pull water through the jet engine

intake–the opening through which water is pulled into the engine

jet propulsion–power made by pushing water or air out the back of an engine

PFD (personal flotation device)–a piece of equipment that protects the pilot and keeps the pilot afloat

plane–to slide across the surface of the water

rudder–a flat, upright piece at the back of a boat used to turn the boat

slalom racing–piloting a boat around buoys set out to form a zigzag course

steering nozzle–a control for the stream of water used to power and steer a jet watercraft

submarine–a move in which the pilot drives the nose of the boat under water

wetsuit–a close-fitting suit that traps water against the skin. The body warms this water and it protects the wearer from cold outside the suit.

wipeout–a fall from the boat, usually when turning or when hit by a wave

To Learn More

Read:

Harris, Jack C. *Personal Watercraft.* Mankato, MN: Crestwood House, 1988.

Italia, Bob. *Jet Skiing.* Minneapolis: Abdo & Daughters, 1991.

Photo Credits:

Index